T0208950

Musings to Meaning

Christina Rosenthal

BALBOA.PRESS
A DIVISION OF HAY HOUSE

Balboa Press books may be ordered through booksellers or by contacting:

Balboa Press
A Division of Hay House
1663 Liberty Drive
Bloomington, IN 47403
www.balboapress.com
1 (877) 407-4847

Print information available on the last page.

ISBN: 978-1-9822-3895-7 (sc)
ISBN: 978-1-9822-3896-4 (e)

Balboa Press rev. date: 01/22/2020

for my children and grandchildren
and anyone seeking inner peace

Contents

Welcome

There is a Voice inside of us. A quiet still Voice that when we give It our attention, we can hear It...feel It....sense It. As we hush our mind's incessant chatter and sit and be still, the Voice emerges.

It gives us guidance, a new idea, comfort, an answer to our questioning. The Voice is forever present. The more interested we are in the Voice, the more It speaks to us. We can even partner with the Voice in delightful co-creation.

This Voice is Love. It is God. It is Spirit. It is Jeshua. It is your favorite Archangel. It is Soul Self. It is Divine Self. It is Oneness. It is All That Is. It is Holy Spirit. It is Source. Whomever your chosen Voice is, It brings into your being inner peace, a feeling of warm contentment, a knowing of Its truth.

The Voice is a steadfast forever friend. The mere focus on the Voice, the stronger It comes into our awareness. This attention to the Voice allows for discernment, a recognizing of the difference between the quiet pure Voice and the loud little voice that always seems to have something to say that has nothing to do with joyning, with peace, with love.

In the times when we feel stuck, in the times when we are at a loss of what and who to believe, in the times when we don't know what is real and what is not, the Voice in us will speak Its loving assurance.

The Voice gives us a go-to place to grow a trusting and exploring of life without limitations, a life without judgments, a life with a sustaining joy.

Musings is my sharing of the Voice that comes to me and through me. As you read each page, perhaps Your Voice will come to you and through you to joyfully jump on the adjoining pages.

Come JOYn with me !

Clarification of Terms

EGO

....the temporary part of us that comes with the body and is about separation and conflict, and all about experiencing the myriad forms of fear. It is the part that is an illusion to God.

SPIRIT, SELF

....the Eternal part of us that is Real, the part of us that Creates, and is all about expressing the unlimited forms of Love. It is the part of us that has never left God.

GOD

....is used interchangeably with One, Spirit, Universe, Oneness, Love, Divine, the Voice, Friends in Upper Realms, Holy Spirit and All That Is.

The principles of **A Course in Miracles** are interwoven throughout these musings, although the soothing, clarifying, unconditionally loving philosophy is known at the center core of our being.

METHINKS

musings while meditating

My Methinks

The world reflects my every thought

My every feeling

And sends it back to me

As experience

My Methinks

Without valuing guilt

Judgment seems useless

And fear unfathomable

My Methinks

I AM

I AM BLESSED

I AM PURIFIED

I AM LOVED

I AM

Close eyes. Speak slowly. Repeat often.

My Methinks

When something is right for you
Truly right for the truth of who you are
It is truly right for all concerned

The Universe is very economical that way

My Methinks

Methinks when enough of us

Have achieved inner peace

The world will change without a fuss

And wars will simply cease

My Methinks

Noisy ego pushes us to believe
Our differences mean incompatibility
So judging must surely follow

That same ego is the one who fears
We will recall it is our diversity
That surely secures our equality

My Methinks

Our outer world reflects our inner world
It's not the other way around

Practicing this will give us an inkling
Of the power of our own inner thinking

My Methinks

Love is ubiquitous
There is no where It is not
It is in every tree and every rock
In every shoe and every sock
In every sunbeam and rain drop
In every line and every dot
It is in every here and every there
In every one and every where
Love is in all
No exceptions

My Methinks

When I let go of my resistances
I let go of my limitations.
Think about that.
Apply.
Repeat.

(not that it's easy, it's just that it's true)

My Methinks

Methinks separation is the experience
Of leaving the God Part of us behind

My Methinks

When I just be

Calm with no distractions

The presence of the Divine

Appears in warm awareness

Revealing It is ever present

Awaiting me to just Be

My Methinks

I am the embodiment of discipline

And in my discipline I find my divinity

And in my divinity all I see are deities

My Methinks

Discover who you are
So you can Know who you are
So you can Honor who you are

And can Create who YOU want to be!

My Methinks

At the center core of our being
Is the truth of what we are...
LOVE
And all of Love's expressions live
Right there too....
strength, kindness, caring,
generosity, compassion,
gentleness, faith, integrity,
confidence, trust, joyfulness,
patience, defenselessness,
peacefulness, and.....
I'm sure you can think of a few more
That are right inside of you!

My Methinks

You cannot know
Of your own sacredness
Without seeing it in others

My Methinks

What we see on the inside
We will see on the outside

What we think on the inside
We will see on the outside

What we believe on the inside
We will see on the outside

What we deny on the inside
We will still see on the outside

Willing to live from the inside out?

My Methinks

What would I do without you?
My indispensable friend
You, on whom I could depend
You've been there all the way through

When I wouldn't know what to do
When I couldn't know how to be
When I didn't comprehend me
And weren't even aware of you

You taught me follow Love, lose fear
Be kind and gentle to all I see
To cherish, believe, be true to me
You have always been forever near

How I grew to love you
To listen, to know your Voice
My Inner Spirit Voice
I know I will never be without You!

My Methinks

When we have accepted

All we have attracted to us

Without any judgment

We will begin to experience

The flow of forgiveness

My Methinks

Valuing judgment begets
Lots of opportunities to judge

But when I pretend that having
Negative opinions are not an option
My mind is full of spaciousness

Sometimes I fill it with compassion

My Methinks

To know of my Wholeness

I need but allow the parts of me
I hid long ago and yesterday

To come into the Light for me
To welcome in a gentle embrace

MERRIMENTS

moments that make us smile

My Merriments

When a lovely sunny day
Happens your way...
Smile
When a cloudy rainy day
Happens your way...
Smile
It's not the kind of day
That matters...
It's the smile

My Merriments

The Highest in ourselves

Is a limitless realm

Shall we meet there

And JOYn as One?

My Merriments

We are holy in so many ways
We are human in so many ways
The wondrous with the weakness
Allowing for both in me and in you
Allows the wonderment of Love

My Merriments

The more I BE the easier I DO

My Merriments

When I smile Love shows up
And all the nothingness
I have been thinking
Disappears

My Merriments

The most beautiful thing
In the world to me
Is to know without a shadow of a doubt
That not being an eternal Spirit
And not having the total support
Of All That Is...
Is not and never can be an option

My Merriments

As I embrace my mistakes
They weaken and wither into nothingness
As the effulgence of love
Rises out of the abyss

My Merriments

Once upon a time
There was only Light
Once upon a time
There was only Love
Once upon a time
There was no time
Once upon a time
Can be now

My Merriments

One summer Sunday I was attending a classical music performance in a refurbished barn in the bucolic rural hills in Upstate New York with about 200 other people. The acclaimed pianist and violinist were about to begin when a cell phone went off in the audience.

You could sense the silent disapproval from all of us. Without delay the violinist played the phone's exact notes! Everyone chuckled. Tension turned into tranquil. Judgment turned into jovial.

We have that same power. Can we not turn our tensions and judgments into light-heartedness? What merry melodies we shall play!

My Merriments

Every cell in my being is Pure Light
And when I place my attention on that
Each cell expands into more Pure Light
Spreading outward to touch
Another Pure Light
I think it was you

My Merriments

Can you say yes to life?
Yes to Love? Yes to joy?
Yes to peace?
Yes to well-being?
Yes to what is?

Maybe yes is the opposite of resistance
How much yes-ness is in you?

My Merriments

I am Spirit
Be not deceived
By the body you see
I am Spirit
Wild, wonderful and free
And so are you
Come, play with me!

My Merriments

Seek the Essence of your Soul Self
The Self that resides deep inside
That is gentle and genuine
Playful and patient
Compassionate and passionate
Wise with wonderment
And knows of no limitations
And share that Essence with another

My Merriments

Grace

If you would ask me
For what I am most grateful
Grace would be my answer

It is Grace that shows me
Love is reality
Fear is not

It is Grace that enables me
To forgive all in me
That is not love

It is Grace that enables me
To allow miracles
Into my life

My most sincere gratefulness
Is the limitless Grace
Available to me...
And to you

My Merriments

Doing my Best
Used to mean efforting,
Producing, and achieving.
Now happily Best means
BE Still Time.

My Merriments

As my Soul and Spirit merge
What and Who they create
Is the wondrous expansion of Love

My Merriments

As our inner Joy grows
So does the heart
Fill with a radiance
That cannot be concealed

My Merriments

Won't it be fun when we align
Who we think we are with
Who we really are!
Who will we be then?

My Merriments

Let us pursue the highest in ourselves
Let us lose interest in what no longer serves us
Let compassion be our chosen companion
Let us see Spirit in everyone we meet
Let us enjoy Who we are becoming

My Merriments

God is Love

Love does not judge

Love does not demand

Love does not see error

Love does not foster fear

Love just Loves

MESSAGES

from

My Team

the Ones I lean on, go to, count on

which include but are not limited to

Jeshua, Holy Spirit, St. Germain, Archangel Chamuel

My Messages

I asked for assistance with learning how to just BE:

The who I am while dreaming is not who I am awake. The who I am awake looks at who I was in the dream with interest, curiosity. But there is no attachment to who I was in the dream or to its contents.

It is the same. Who I am in this world is not Who I Am awake. The Who I Am awake looks at who I am in the world with interest, curiosity. But there is no attachment to who I am in the world or to its contents.

My Messages

I asked my Team: tell me what its like?

Like you, we have our jobs to do.

What is that?

To be God expanded.

Do you/I have a choice in how we be God expanded?

You/We are to be Love in every moment of now.

As I focused I felt the fullness of a Golden Love. But as my focus waned, I said: that is easier for You.

Yes, but We are here for you. You are not alone.

I felt Their envelopment of me...Their Presence... Their support....Their assurance.

My Messages

I earnestly want to be Love, so one morning I asked my Team if I were learning about Love.

Allow the Love We have for you to penetrate. You keep It separate still. Let It in. It is who you are, who We are. Feel what you truly are. You are free to do that. Free not to monitor the amount of love you accept.

Then I will lose myself!

Precisely. You will find your Self. You will lose the self that is not you and find the Self that is.

A couple of mornings later I reached out to Them. Since I am invested in my little self, how do I lose interest in that part of me?

First, be gentle with yourself. Second, focus on the You that is part of Us. The more you focus on the You that is Love, the more Love you will let in. And the more Your Self you will become.

My
Messages

Once when I had been stuck in judgment and doubt I asked a question: how can I keep from getting stuck?

The answer came so quickly: *NON-ATTACHMENT.*

I was focusing on what that meant when They spoke again:

If you are going down the river in a boat and you think the boat is keeping you safe, that's attachment.

While I am marveling at this metaphor, They spoke once more:

When you realize you ARE the boat, you ARE the current, you ARE the river, you ARE the wind; when you realize you are all of it, there will be no attachment......there will be no fear, no stuckness of any kind.

My Messages

One day I wanted to know how I can grow my trust.

As you think of trusting Us, know that your Real You is with Us.....orchestrating your life, right along with Us.

Hmmm.....makes it seem easier to trust, somehow.

My Messages

Of high priority on the evolutionary journey to my Self, is the accepting of what is, to not resist what happens. So when I went for a dental appointment for the third time in as many weeks, I was expecting to have a new crown put in place of the temporary crown. Easy. Breezey.

But when the crown was tested, it was a misfit and I was told they would have to re-do the tedious work of exposing the gum. I felt like bolting. Why is this happening? No way. How can this be?

Instead of a smiley, short dental visit, the next hour was exasperatingly painful, followed by uncomfortable pain the remaining of the day.

So the following morning as I began my quiet meditative time, I expressed my upset, not about enduring more pain, but having so much resistance when presented with the necessary re-do.

Seems you are resisting that you were resistant?

Yes.

See the silly?

Aaaaahh. Letting go of resistance is like sinking into a warm bubblebath.

My
Messages

The Course* invites us to value nothing of this world.

So I ask how can I lose interest in valuing?

Something is either Love or nothing.
If it is LOVE,
Smile.
If it is nothing,
Forgive it.

**A Course in Miracles*

My Messages

Wanting clarification and understanding about forgiveness:

Forgiveness is non-judgment
Non-judgment is acceptance
Acceptance is non-resistance
Non-resistance is allowing
Allowing is receiving
Receiving is God-expanded.

I was so excited. You mean forgiveness begets non-judgement and non-judgment becomes acceptance and.........

NO! .....was the loud interruption.

Forgiveness IS non-judgment
Non-judgment IS acceptance
Acceptance IS non-resistance
Non-resistance IS allowing
Allowing IS receiving
Receiving IS God-expanded.

Now I was really excited! You mean it's all the same? Acceptance is receiving.......and......non-judgment is God-expanded.......and......
Yes, it is all the same, was the firm but gentle reply.

My Messages

I want to know more about being God expanded. How do I do that?

No doing. Being. Recognize that you are God expanded and nothing else. The less something else you are, the more room God has to expand in you.

How do I BE that?

Trust that leaves no room for fear.

My Messages

I was asking my Team how my Soul Self saw me and was shown a sphere with white light and greys, so I asked is this how You see me?

NO, this is how We see you.

And They were gone....till I realized the next moment that They were <u>in</u> me. There was no separation. I was enjoying the bright light feeling when They added....

When you see yourself as your mistakes or your judgments, it pushes Us out of the way. We cannot be in that same space.

I then saw that They were not in the grey areas.

My Messages

One meditation I asked Archangel Chamuel, who has been with me for a long long time..... What is it that you actually do for me? Do you wait for me to call on you? Do you hold the space for me? Are you always available? Do you teach me about love?

I be that which I am which makes it easier for you to be that which you are.

My
Messages

One morning it was as if They were waiting for me to meditate.

How are you doing?

Good.

How are you feeling?

Fine.

About your past?

I'm not feeling any attachment.

About your future?

hmmm....I'm not feeling any attachment to that either.

Your past and your future have a direct link. Not letting go of all of the parts of your past that you judge as having made poor choices, will be reflected in your worry and projected into your future. As you forgive the past, you let go of the future without even conceptualizing it.

I was with this for a while. Then I told them I loved Them All so much.

You cannot love Us unless you love you....all of you, not just parts of you.

I think I got it.

Yes, and We are here to help you maintain it.

My Messages

When I had been concerned about some physical issues I was having:

It is the removal of old. Let go of anything and everything in the past....so the body will not need to store any unforgiveness.

My Messages

Feeling the need and the desire to have more strength in being a Light in the world. I asked how I could achieve more consistency.

The strength is in the trust. The more you trust the more there is for you. We have so much to give you. Judge no thing, no one. We are taking care of everything. Stay steadfast. Your steadfastness assists in bringing the Light into the world.

My
Messages

I was feeling my typical upset about the corruption in government. I could sense that the Fear is fighting for survival. So I went into meditation and I could feel Them.

It's all right to feel the confusion. Don't be afraid. You are not forgotten. The dimensions are shifting. Stay strong. Be in your purity. The Pure is permeating everywhere.

My Messages

Having been upset and judging some responses to a high profile racist court case, I went into my morning meditation. I began by saying good morning to the Essence of all my cells and atoms and electrons.

Your judging against them effects us.

Why?

They are you also......why do you not judge us?

You are part of me.

So are they......judge them not, for they know not what they do. You have been them too. Forgive. You have been everyone. Everyone has been you. There is only Oneness. Forgive. Nothing is happening.
LOVE....so something can happen.

My
Messages

Getting that my purpose was taking me on a new path:

There are things for you to accomplish that can't be done with your busyness. The accomplishments are not about doing. But being.

Practice being in Spirit. You can be in action from a place of being or you can be in action from a place of doing. One is from the Spirit. The other is from the ego.

My Messages

Wanting to know about loving and being loved:

You are so totally and unconditionally loved. We love all with all love, and when anyone will hear Us, We speak.

I want to love all with all love.

Your Spirit Self, the Real You, already does.

Can this me love all with all love?

The more you focus on your Spirit Self or One of Us, the more Love your little me becomes.

So I give Spirit Self and You attention, think about You and my Spirit Self and You will merge into me?

How does it feel to imagine You and Us merging into you?

Soft. Powerful. Love-filled. Expansive.

Your imagining is real. Repeat often.

My Messages

Talking to my Team one day: You have said that in order for me to be whole, I need to accept all of me. But my errors, regrets, anything I perceive as dark, are all illusions, not real, You have also said. So how do I accept the illusions as part of me and my wholeness?

As you embrace all that you perceive as dark and therefore not real, your embracing of all of it transforms it all into Love. And Love is your wholeness.

My Messages

How do I become the observer and not judge?

When you know all of it is not real.

How can I know all of it is not real?

When you experience you are Spirit.

How can I experience I am Spirit?

Be still.

MEANDERINGS

wanderings and wonderings

My Meanderings

Whither I go or whither I stay
Whither I wander to one's dismay
It matters not where I be
There is ONE who resides in me
ONE who sticks like glue
Even when I haven't a clue
So whither I go or whither I stay
The ONE will be there anyway

My Meanderings

We could always click our heels and go home

But don't we love the yellow brick road?

My Meanderings

On one snowy spring day...

The buds were determined to sprout
Even in the adverse weather

So we too have been known to sprout
In adverse conditions

It strengthens the path to our own powerful Nature

Something the trees have known all along

My Meanderings

What if your name was 'Oneness'
And you met someone
And introduced yourself.
She replied, 'my name is Oneness too'.
Then another joined you.
He said, 'hi...my name is Oneness'.
Shortly, two more people joined you.
Their names were Oneness also.
If everyone's name was Oneness

Then would we begin to get it?

My Meanderings

Walking in the woods one day, I stopped to sit among the trees. In time my gaze looked up at the giant majestic tree in front of me. It was magnificent! .....except for a couple large broken branches that were still attached, hanging lifeless by the tree's stately trunk.

I had the thought, this tree would be so perfect if it weren't for those dead limbs. They should be cut down. Quite suddenly and certainly unexpectedly, I felt the tree respond.

"All of my branches are part of me. I wouldn't be whole without them. They don't diminish my magnificence. They ensure my perfection."

My Meanderings

It matters not who you have been

It matters only who you are becoming

My Meanderings

When will I know I am part of All That Is?
When I've read every bit of the Course x 3?*
When I've forgiven everyone plus me?

Or is it when I summon a little willingness
To allow the Light and the Love of Spirit
To flow into me, through me, merging
With the essence of the Spirit Me
Making all my illusions irrelevant.

**A Course in Miracles*

My Meanderings

Sitting at the computer one morning, I saw a large flying insect that was caught between the screen and the window. I cranked open the window but he held fast to his position on the glass, having no idea he was free.

I thought how stupid that he couldn't see that he was no longer trapped. Couldn't he feel the fresh air awaiting him? All he had to do was let go.

My next thought was I am he and he is me. I do that.....think there is no way out of a belief or situation, stubbornly hold my stance up against a glass wall...... when all I have to do is choose again!

I thanked him as I gently nudged him to freedom.

My Meanderings

When we are young we are taught to stop,
Look, and listen before entering a street.
What a good idea before entering our day!
Stop to be still.
Look within.
Listen to our Eternal Voice.

My Meanderings

Have you seen red buds of maples in early spring?

Have you seen the half moon high in the sky?

Have you seen the Love in the Core of your Soul?

The maples and the moon have.

My Meanderings

If a car needs fuel to get anywhere

Wouldn't that mean that an ego

Needs fear to get anywhere?

My Meanderings

Isn't it my Spirit that is content
And my ego that craves

Isn't it my Spirit that creates
And my ego that struggles

Isn't it my Spirit that trusts
And my ego that doubts

Isn't it my Spirit that is invulnerable
And my ego that fears

Isn't it my Spirit that is REAL.............

My Meanderings

I can see when I am going through life being sore

I can also see when I go through life soaring

Which one will I choose for today?

My Meanderings

The Bible says that as a man thinketh so it is

Quantum Physics says that whether
a wave becomes a particle is
contingent on the observer

I don't know the difference between those two
Can you find one?

My Meanderings

Could Old Souls simply be Souls

Who have not been stuck

In creating the same dramas

Lifetime after lifetime?

My Meanderings

Are you attached to what you are wanting?

Or are you able to want without attachment?

One is scarcity bringing the fear of not having.

The other is abundance allowing the highest.

My Meanderings

When will I get that doubt
Is a form of fear?

When will I get that trust
Is a form of love?

When will I get that the one
I choose is real for me?

When will I get
That I can choose again?

My Meanderings

hmmm……could…….?

Spirit/Soul Self
Created by God in Its Own Image.
The Spirit Self stayed with God.
The Soul Self went on an adventure
To create a Being of Love Expanded.

Ego/(hu)man self
Tacked itself onto the body to attack,
Tempting the Soul Self in an attempt
To believe that separation and fear
Are real and are to be revered.

My Meanderings

Peace
My occasional visitor
My intermittent friend
How may I beckon you
To move in?

Listen, You say
To my Inner Soul
And allow my True Self
To unfold

Then I can have it?
Is that all I do?
My being me will
Lead to You?

I am Peace, You say
And we are One
The journey is complete
That we have begun

My Meanderings

If I may remain in calm peacefulness
While the world is caught in chaos
Might that be expedient
In bringing peace into the world?

MISCHIEFS

might be annoying

My Mischiefs

Wisdom is acquired
By all the decisions
We make in life....
Especially
The stupid ones

My Mischiefs

Did you ever notice
That when you forgive
Something in the past
It stops being a Pest?

The past can't last
Unless we won't forgive it

My Mischiefs

When I get down, it is not long before I ask "Who's in a funk?"

My Spirit Self says, "Not me. I don't do funks!"

My little ego self says, "Too bad. I like funks."

Thanks for the clarification, little ego self. "Go take a nap!"

And with that I begin feeling
Funkless and fearless!

My Mischiefs

When we realize we are part of All That Is
We will see that pondering unworthiness
Is just plain arrogance

My Mischiefs

The Course* says......

Everything is in right order

No matter how things may look

So we might as well forgive it all

And just go write a book

*A Course in Miracles

My Mischiefs

See my error
Own my error
Forgive my error
Transmute my error
Into air!

My
Mischiefs

One winter storm left tree branches covered with thick ice. Branches that didn't break, bent low with the glistening weight. The ice covered trees lasted 4 days before temperatures rose enough to free the laden limbs.

That day I was walking up the shortcut trail back to my house. I watched in wonder as the branches of small yellow beech trees blew freely in the wind. So I remarked "aren't you glad you are at last free from the heavy ice?" Shockingly, they replied, "it doesn't matter".

This has a profoundly deep meaning for me: To equally accept the burdens and the blessings. With no resistance to either, accepting what is.

My
Mischiefs

Ego never forgives.
Ego only pretends to forgive.
But our Spirit Self
Loves to radiate from within
And suddenly forgiveness
Becomes a given.

My Mischiefs

If non-attachment is a pre-requisite
For inner peace
I'm attached to achieving
Non-attachment

My ego loves a conundrum

My Mischiefs

Formula:

Have a regret

Forgive the regret

See the disappearance of the effects of the regret

Be happy

My Mischiefs

Fear used to run me

Now it just walks me

I'm even learning to put fear on a leash

So it can go only so far before I yank it in

And choose again

My Mischiefs

During a psycho-spiritual workshop, I asked everyone to go out in the surrounding nature and connect with one part of nature. Focus for a few minutes. Notice what that part of nature has that you would like to develop in yourself.

I too did the assignment, deciding to focus on a big billowy white cloud passing by. I marveled at how it went with the wind without a trace of resistance. I wanted to develop that ability to go with the flow, accepting what is, going with the current. As I meditated on the cloud, I could feel the essence of the cloud enter me.

When everyone returned to share their experience, they were all similar to mine. Whatever part of nature they chose, they found something they wanted to develop in themselves. Then they too felt the essence of their chosen nature enter into them.

Want to try it?

My Mischiefs

Pure One

I'm talkin' to you
Who do you think you are
Your mistakes?
Your regrets?
Not a chance!
You are Pure One
Just like the rest of us

My
Mischiefs

Ain't nothin' gonna happen to us

That our Soul Self didn't

Help to orchestrate

My Mischiefs

Authenticity

Is it me?
Or am I hiding
In whom I please?

Is it worth
The price I pay
Just to be
A cast of clay?

For both of us
Not to know
The essence, the wonder
The Being in my Soul?

Isn't it lamentable
That we would rather see
My many masks
In lieu of me?

Shh...I hear a Voice
Beckoning, be still
A still Inner Voice
Be real, be real, be real

My Mischiefs

Deciding who to listen to

My little self (ego)

Or my Magnificent Self (Spirit)

Depends on which one I want

To know better

My Mischiefs

When Light enters dark
Dark cannot exist
When Love enters fear
Fear cannot exist

Makes you want to choose
Light and Love, doesn't it?

My Mischiefs

My body is the perfect
Mask for perceiving

That I am different and
Separate from you

But it is still just a mask

My Mischiefs

It is only my ego

That can carry

A grievance

Into the now

My Mischiefs

Since we are created in God's image
We are Love
Should we not act like it?

MISHAPS

when wishing it weren't

My Mishaps

When I am feeling insecure
There is a go-to-place I hold dear

I call on Friends in Upper Realms
They're sure to come and calm me down

To remind me how They reside inside
Fully present to comfort and to guide

When I can remember this for sure
I know I will cease to feel insecure

My Mishaps

When we're so sure things have to be one way
We can be sure we need to get out of the way

And allow Spirit to have a say and tell us
Turn things over and stop all the fuss

So when we think there is only one solution
We can surely know we are in delusion

My Mishaps

When it is difficult to trust

That mishaps turn into miracles

Follow your heart into the impossible

Walk the peaceful path of lucent Light

Into the wonder of the Oneness

My Mishaps

There is always a bigger picture

No matter what the facts may be

There is a vision beyond what we can see

Facts are not reality, neither lack nor time

There is a bigger picture that will unfurl

In the realm of Love's reality

My Mishaps

Forgiving someone for something
That occurred in the past
Transforms our present.

We no longer live in the result
Of what occurred.
That is the power of forgiveness.

It doesn't change that it happened
But it changes the effects of what happened.
Every time.

My Mishaps

It's hard to give up things we're good at
Like blaming others or faulting ourselves.
And we've done this for oh sooo long
It's hard to give up things to which we
Have achieved such a degree of proficiency.
Agreed?

My Mishaps

If I want the acceptance and freedom
To trust what I wish to believe,
Should not I give that same
Acceptance and freedom
To others to trust what they wish to believe?

I'll have to work on that.
You too?

My
Mishaps

My ego has worries
Of pain and suffering
Of having enough
Of regrets and grievances
Of the past and the future

My Spirit feels
Safe and unconcerned
Timeless and joyful
Peaceful and loving
And has compassion
For the one who worries

My Mishaps

In lieu of attempting to convert and convince

A little willingness to understand and appreciate

Will also bring a willingness for healing solutions

Whether with your self or another

My Mishaps

If you knew that you could choose
Never to have to suffer again,
Would you?
Pain comes with having a human body
Suffering is the result of resisting the pain

My Mishaps

When I judge
I am attacking

When I am attacking
I attack me

When I attack me
I get hurt

Why would I ever think
Judging is worth it!

My
Mishaps

When someone we love leaves this world
Isn't it comforting to know they have returned
To the world of Oneness
Where there is no separation
Where they also are not separate from us
Nor can they be?

My Mishaps

We speak of death
We cannot die
We release the temporary vessel
For our eternal Soul Self
Who then is but being birthed
Birthed into blissful freedom
Back into unifying Oneness

My Mishaps

Whatever my thoughts, emotions, and beliefs
The ones that take away my peace
I am so very grateful that no matter what
I think and feel and believe
The Spirit Me has never left God
The same is true for you, you know

My Mishaps

Justification and stubbornness go together
I doubt you can find one without the other
When I'm so right with my opinions
I assume my perceptions have dominion
I have no interest in validating your stance
And take no notice in a harmonious dance
I'll defend to the end and not budge a bit
Until I realize it is with fear I sit
Then I know to be still, invite Spirit in to clear
So I may Love again

My Mishaps

Are you resisting what is?
Fatigue and powerlessness are sure to follow

Are you accepting what is?
Vitality and creativity are sure to follow

My Mishaps

When I am wishing it weren't

When I am wishing what is, isn't

Or wishing I could turn back time

To redo, re-say, omit, commit

Forgetting that in forgiving it all

There'll be no need to wish it weren't

My
Mishaps

When we hang onto anger
Revenge, attack, condemnation
We hang onto littleness
No matter its seemingly looming size
It is all still littleness
When we return into our Spirit Self
Willing to have Spirit's perspective
Our inner peace becomes essential
And the looming littleness goes away

My Mishaps

How can the world be such a mess
When there is the beauty of a summer day
How can I deem fears magnifying
When there is chirping chatter high in the trees
How can I feel hopelessness abounds
When there is a deer staring at me

My Mishaps

What we value we will experience

When we value guilt, it's happy to show up for us
When we value judgment, it's glad to give us the opportunity
When we value fear, it's delighted to manifest fear at every turn

When we value joy, it's happy to show up for us
When we value peace, it's glad to give us the opportunity
When we value love, it's delighted to create love at every turn

MAYBES

potentials, possibles, probables

My Maybes

What if we are well on our way

To losing interest in harmfulness

In any form?

My Maybes

What if transparency

Is an up-and-coming value

For more and more of us?

My
Maybes

What if the planet has decided

Along with us that we now want

To experiment with a higher dimension

A higher vibration than third dimension?

My Maybes

What if at the center core of our being

Is Love and nothing else

So that fear is just something we made up

And can choose to lose?

My Maybes

What if the feeling of gratefulness

Is the easiest way to hasten

More to be grateful for?

My Maybes

What if miracles

Are meant to be

An every day in every way

Occurrence?

My Maybes

What if suffering feels real

When we resist our pain

And disappears when we accept our pain?

My Maybes

What if there is a new you

Unfolding each and every day

Allowing you to choose anew

The one you are becoming?

My Maybes

What if we are in fact

Part of All That Is

Not separate from God

Except in our minds?

My Maybes

What if Jeshua brought us

A Course in Miracles

To correct the misconceptions

Of Christianity?

My Maybes

What if when we die

We are actually

Being birthed?

My Maybes

What if there is no real difference

Between quantum physics

And spirituality?

My
Maybes

What if we can create from a place of Being

By knowing that the doing is done?

My Maybes

What if our living in inner peace

Brings peace into the world?

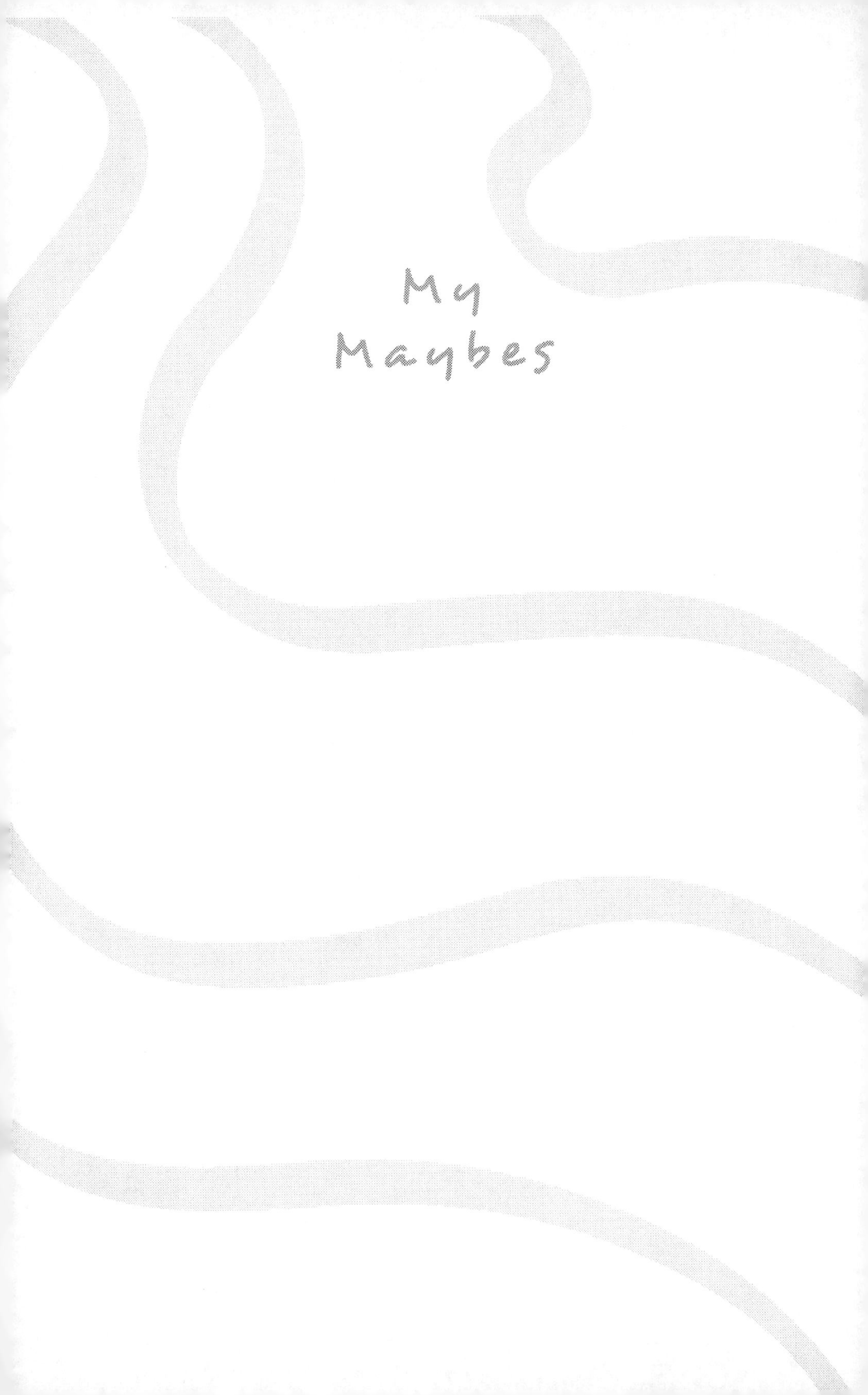

My Maybes

What if we didn't come here to champion

Forms of fear, rather we came here to be a

Powerful loving creative force?

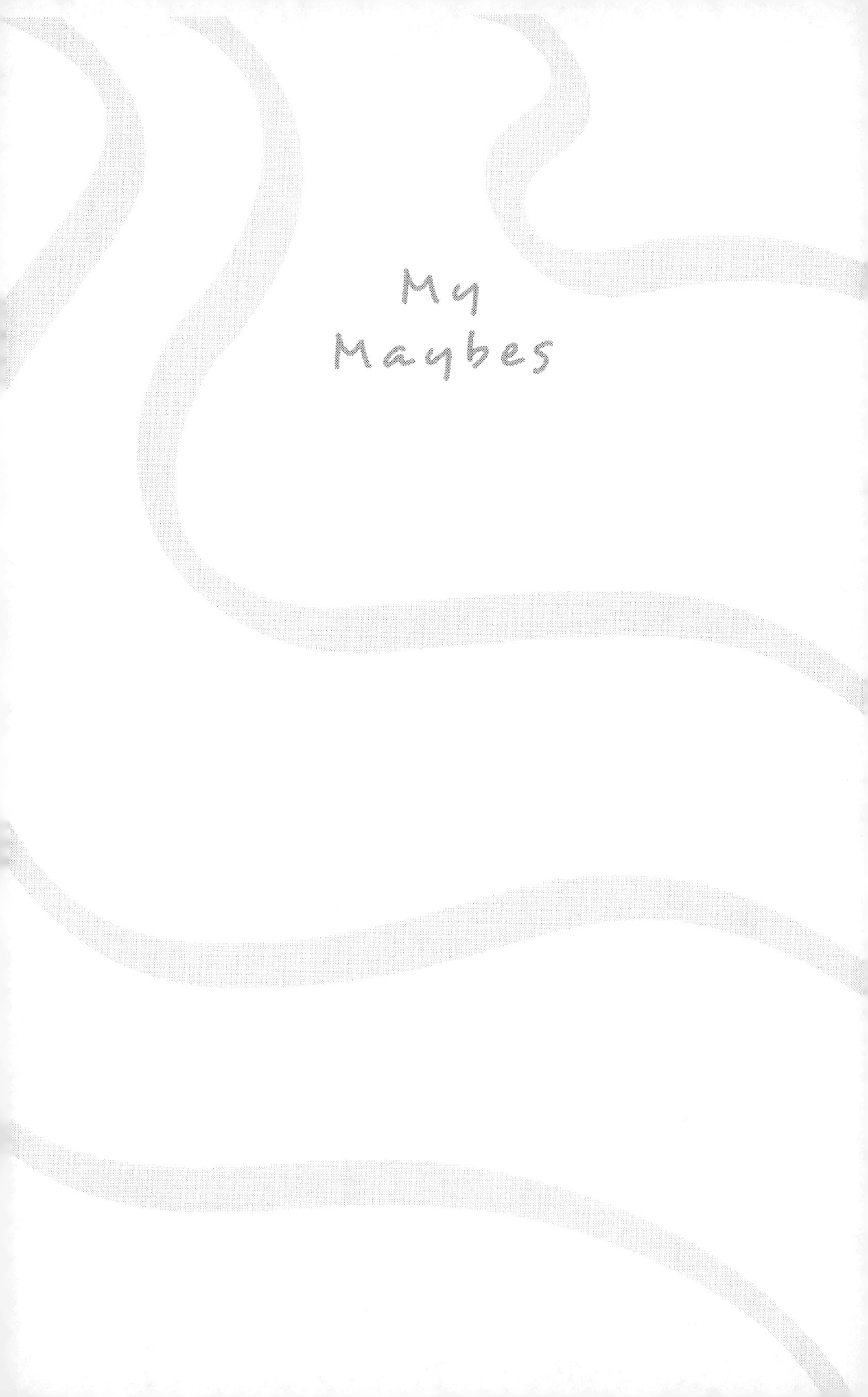
My
Maybes

What if to see the holiness in someone else

I must first see it in myself?

My Maybes

What if our outer world

Reflects our inner world

So that changing our inner thoughts

Will change our outer world reality?

My
Maybes

What if when I embrace the me

That has made mistakes

All that is left is the embrace?

My
Maybes

What if when I perceive guilt as a thing of Value, I perceive guilt in everyone else?

My
Maybes

What if we are making all of this up?

IN APPRECIATION

I am immeasurably grateful to Jeshua and to the Holy Spirit for bringing these spiritual truths into my life and into the world. I have thoroughly enjoyed the co-creation of *Musings.*

Printed in the United States
By Bookmasters